Prison Possibilities
Voluntary Exile

Concept

Rev. Mike Wanner

Copyright Rev. Mike Wanner, February 25, 2017

Selected Images Used by License

Table Of Contents

Table Of Contents 3
Introduction 4
- What Is a Voluntary Exile? 5
- Why I am Writing This Book 6
- Prisoner Profiles 7
- "Prisoner Profile Bureaus 8
- Prison Rehabilitation Limitations 9
- A Brief on A New Path 11
- "Prisoners Can Contribute and Evolve 12
- "What Rights Would a Prisoner Be Willing To Trade for What Benefits? 13
- "Would Prisoners Surrender Citizenship For Freedom? 14
10 - "My Ideas Are Seeds, You Can Be A Farmer 15
11 - Sentence Transfers 16
12 - No Cancellation 17
13 - Declarations To Be Considered For Both Countries 18
14 - Thank You 19
16 - Can You Help Community Service 22
17 - Can You Help Communication 23
18 - Don't Worry Ever 24
19 - Resource List 25
20 - Angels Please Prayers 27
21 - Private Channeling 28
22 - Reverend Mike Wanner 29

Introduction

I invite every reader to consider the ideas that can create freedom for taxpayers from the extreme costs of imprisoning huge numbers of our fellow citizens. We have taken for granted that we somehow can afford these costs.

Alas and unfortunately, the costs of incarceration are about to eat up the quality of the American Dream. We are all gradually being banished to involuntary servitude to our insecurities.

Yes, we are threatened by great evil in the world. There is no need for us to overreact. There is some justification for the restrictions that are imposed upon those who have been convicted of a crime.

As taxpayers, we in the greater community have an interest in how our tax dollars are spent. Incarceration is a huge expense and if there were unlimited funds in our national budgets there would be no need to consider changing anything unless fairness was a prominent goal.

Unfortunately, national budgets around the world are stretched by government expenditures and it may make sense for us to evaluate the reasonableness of our expenses. We could find there are little opportunities for prudence.

We could also find that there are options not yet considered. This book is an invitation to look at what we are doing related to incarceration and see what we find.

1 - What Is a Voluntary Exile?

With this writing, I am proposing a radical shift for us. While exile has happened before, this proposal lays out an agreement for a voluntary structuring which could bring great freedom to taxpayers.

I continue to start discussions about things that could make a difference in the relationship between the jailed and the jailers and everybody else involved with either group of people. It seems that little has changed for a long time and it may be time to analyze what is and change it to what was or what could be.

Density of humans within a confined space can lead to a tension that can at times be unhealthy. Prisons seem to accentuate the negative and complicate constructive relationships.

If we can send people to a place that they would rather be and close the door to those no longer wanting to be with us while we have truncated the costs to our taxpayers then we have taken control and chosen wisely.

Disclaimer

I the author, am not involved with prisons or prisoners but am sharing what is coming to me in an effort to spread understanding and trigger conversation that can be helpful. It may be that the discussion needs finessing and I invite your wisdom in the mix.

2 - Why I am Writing This Book

I hope that this book continues the work started by my other books and continues to enhance the lives of Prison Employees, Prisoners, Taxpayers and the Families of Each of these groups.

As I have been writing my early books on the subject of Prisons, the complexity of the process has been amazing to me.

The books that I have previously published so far about the prison situations are:

Angel Raphael Speaks Volume 4: Angels, Addicts, Alcoholics & Prisoners – Oh Yeah!
Angel Raphael Speaks Volume 5: Prisoners Caring for Alcoholics - Australia In Miniature Projects Intro
Angel Raphael Speaks Volume 6: Prisoners Caring for Addicts Australia In Miniature For Addicts
Prison Jobs Now: Providing Care For Addicts And Alcoholics
Angel Raphael Speaks - Prisons (A small Kindle only book)
Contained Care Communities: Concept
Australia In Miniature Projects
Prison Possibilities Dialogue Series: Concept
Prison Possibilities Dialogue Series: Volume 2 Dialogues
Prison Possibilities Dialogue Series: Volume 3 Dialogues
Prison Possibilities Dialogue Series: Volume 4 Dialogues
Prison Possibilities Dialogue Series: Volume 5 Dialogues

3 - Prisoner Profiles

In *Prison Possibilities Dialogue Series: Volume 3 Dialogues*, I proposed a business enterprise be created to write, post and share prisoner profiles so that people outside the prison system could shop for skills within the system of prisoners who were looking for skills that prisoners had.

That type of service could be particularly useful for international individuals who needed to access talent but lacked the resources to hire from the international community of skill holders.

Prisoner profile formats could vary from bureau to bureau but they should at least include:
1. Credit Report
2. Educational Report
3. Criminal Record
4. Skills and Certifications
5. Family History and obligations.
6. Children and spouses
7. Prisoner performance during incarceration
8. Any Violence History

I will post Dialogue 26 "Prison Profile Bureaus" from *Prison Possibilities Dialogue Series: Volume 3 Dialogues* in the next chapter.

4 - "Prisoner Profile Bureaus
[Dialogue 26]

A New Business Opportunity may be to create a Prisoner Profile Bureau if that is legal and proper to do so. Check out the legality first.

The idea is that many prisoners could benefit from the availability of a publicly available profile on as many aspects of their life as make sense for potential employers. What kind of products to create and who should pay for them are not my concern at this time but the value of such a service could be big.

This idea would only be successful if the orchestrator of the process has sufficient credibility to present themselves to the public as an objective credible resource. My thinking is that this could be a sideline for credit bureaus or it could be a government service or government subsidized service to increase the likelihood that those discharged can stay out. Family status could help to show that the one discharged has the motivation to do a good and credible job.

Skills and capabilities and certifications can help to target an audience for the bureau and increase the value of profiles for the one discharged. The intent of the service would be to qualify great candidates for great companies so that the prisoner can find a great job and the employer a great and long lasting employee. In that process, the community can have more productivity, less prisoners, more workers and less prison costs."

5 - Prison Rehabilitation Limitations

The Title of this chapter and content to follow comes directly from Angel Raphael Speaks Message Set 10 because it sets the stage for the reasoning behind part of the exile idea. I swap content in and out because I do not expect readers to read all my books in order to follow my concepts and understand exactly what I am saying about a particular facet that I am writing about in the moment.

"Prison Rehabilitation

The answer to prison rehabilitation is purpose. While some institutions may have initiated programs to engage their residents, the feeling of a purposeful life brings a new reality to the incarcerated.

Purposes to consider will be ones that work for the incarcerated as well as the society which actually pays the bills. Special characteristics to include would be the creation of a feeling of accomplishment generated by prisoner effort and drastic cost savings for the institution.

The real loss to prisons is wasted time, no productivity and no graciousness of interactive genius. If invited, the right use of time can provide different results than now seen….

..The best way to learn about what is possible is to listen to the troubled stories of the incarcerated people. Their genius can be tapped by mining information about how to fill the gap that they slipped in to so that newer walkers on their path can find the gap filled by their charity of sharing their pain as a love patch to the sink holes of society.

The answers through this channel are coming differently than most could conceive and that is because neither you nor I have a job whose agenda has its own needs…

…Their opportunities are paramount in the areas of personal safety for all and the possibility to create new meaningful arrangements that are self-sustaining for all levels of the resident base and those employed in the industry. " ARS 10

BUT

What is possible for prisoners with life sentences? It seems that the doors for purpose and rehabilitation are closed.

Containing the prisoner for public safety is a worthy goal. Spending taxpayers dollars to do that is a community problem.

Money spent on prisons is not available for education and other community service or care programs. This book invites the consideration of exiling prisoners who would prefer to leave this country, surrender their citizenship and eliminate themselves from us supporting them

6 - A Brief on A New Path

Like all the books in my current prison books, this book will be deliberately brief for a number of reasons. The intensity of the ideas and thought streams that are coming to me will serve best if they can be integrated and there needs to be enough space to combine and separate concepts so they can be comprehended.

Moving too fast will be problematic and shift to a complexity that does not serve anybody. Clarity is the goal and that is enhanced when the concept being considered is large enough to focus on but also small enough to not be lost in the process.

A large part of the complexity of prisons is analogous to a tree, where eventually everything matters. When you have a sick branch, the tree will be eventually effected.

When you have a sick tree, the branches can be impacted much quicker because the nutrients for the branches flow through the tree to reach the branches. (This concept is shared for conceptualization only as I have no forestry experience but you can let me know if I am wrong. No worries.)

Using a house analogy, the foundation supports the walls that support the floor above and then the walls above progressively until the roof is finished but then we need to put on a roof so that everything below is protected down to the foundation.

I have shared the tree trunk above and will bring up some example branches in the following chapters but then you will add more and more so the Idea of Exile Possibilities blossoms.

7 - "Prisoners Can Contribute and Evolve
[Dialogue 1]

Each facility has different rules about the rights and movement of Prisoners. I would encourage each prisoner to consider participation to the full extent of their interest, ability and freedom.

Knowing the rules is an important part of all things in which a person participates. Patience will serve prisoners well if they will wait until the time that comments are invited and to what degree participation is unmoderated.

Please know that prison staffs can be flexible like anybody else when the people they are interacting with act in a more peaceful way. I invite you to be aware of the way that other may perceive you.

Human nature is to be reciprocate appropriately so that respectful behavior is reciprocated with respectful behavior. I invite you to realize that patience can serve you well over time.

Please pay attention and see what you can do that will make a difference in small ways. Little changes can add up over time and create new options for all participants.

I have been amazed at the fact that almost always someone will notice changes and ask why. Why leads to further conversation and further understanding and the expansion of possibilities." The dialogue reference that follow are from my books in the *Prison Possibilities Dialogue Series*.

8 - "What Rights Would a Prisoner Be Willing To Trade for What Benefits?
[Dialogue 2]

Prisoners have rights that are protected by the U. S. Constitution. Do you know all your rights? If you have someone dear in prison or jail, you may benefit them by learning what their rights are. There are even some rights before prison. Inmates have some rights to be free, from inhuman conditions that may be seen as "cruel and unusual" punishment.

The laws are old and complicated and I am not qualified to interpret them but therein I think may lie some need for updating or modernization. Yes, it seems that the Americans with Disabilities Act does apply but so do some highly restrictive narrow rules. Yes, they are entitled to adequate medical care also.

And the list goes on but the questions I ask is what laws could be changed to allow prisoners to permanently waive rights.

Releasing institutions from compliance with law is not allowed but changing laws to allow institutional freedom could allow prisoners to surrender their rights and prisons to save money and taxpayers to be taxed less.

The question flows from the original Angel Raphael Speaks Message.

"Prisoner Surrender of Rights

Those interested in any of the concepts shared could also consider surrendering of some rights to further the benefits to the governmental unit. ARS11"

9 - "Would Prisoners Surrender Citizenship For Freedom?
[Dialogue 3]

Prisoners are very expensive to our government and the money spent on their incarceration is not available for programs that benefit other citizens.

If there was a way for prisoners to give up U.S. Citizenship, void all entitlements from all US agencies, surrender their birthrights forever, release Social Security from all or most of their entitlements and forever sever themselves from the United States in return for freedom from jail upon deportation, do you think they or you would go and be free?

Don't pack your bag because this is merely hypothetical but it would be great for the US if we were able to find a country that would be willing to open their doors to the most violent of our inmates. That would be a new version of England/Australia process and totally separate from the Australia in Miniature process that I wrote about. While this is hypothetical, US citizens who have dual citizenship somewhere may be in a better position than most to make this a reality.

If you are or know a prisoner who has family elsewhere in the world, consider all the values of the situation and ask those in a position to do so if they would initiate international political efforts to bargain in behalf of the prisoner. Every situation is different and success at this is unlikely but I invite you to consider all legal possibilities for freedom."

10 - "My Ideas Are Seeds, You Can Be A Farmer
[Dialogue 4]

Reasonable people can assess reality and decide for themselves what might be possible if we avoid all the old structure and streamline the process of creating reasonable options to what we are doing. We are not locked in to the realities of yesterday.

Common Sense is not so common anymore and I invite all leaders to start dialogues that are reasonable, revolutionary, realistic and pursue-able. Why not have a little coffee meeting and talk about simple steps to finding freedom for someone by changing rules that effect many?

I would encourage efforts that are Pro-Bono for the greater good as I expect they can be more productive in a shorter timeline than trying to free a specific person for jaywalking.

A wide brush is great for painting the side of a barn but the effort here is to dot I's and cross T's in a legal document that lets many people free with reasonable rules that change criteria.

The right balance is what you would be wise to pursue but purpose, patience, persistence, politicking and people will be the keys who can open doors for many people. Furthermore, acceleration is furthered by respect for all involved at every level. People are not required to listen to new ideas but usually will if they are objectively and respectfully presented."

11 - Sentence Transfers

The underlying reality is that the value of a candidate for exile must be enough for the country that beckons them to want them enough to put up with the political negotiations. A completed exile could be a big game of chess or a major accomplishment.

The termination of citizenship would leave the exiled prisoner totally at the mercy of the initiating country but that could be awesome also for the exiled one. The appeal for the US is the freedom from the legal responsibilities of supervising, feeding, housing, caring for and protecting the exiled one.

The appeal for the exiled one would be new or renewed freedoms to go many places in the world with the exception of the united states. Lawyers for both sides would need to be very specific so that all parties are protected on paper from all obvious and consequential potentials.

I think it can make a lot of Dollars and Sense for the Federal Government and or the states. I think it can make a lot of sense for the ones exiled also.

12 - No Cancellation

The circumstances of the exile should be clear to all parties that there is to be joint and several termination of all past, present and future connection and access to the United States of America.

Agencies should be involved to the degree necessary to insure that all business matters are finished and terminated forever before the exile is complete.

There will never be another US passport issued to the exiled one.

There will never be another US Visa issued to the exiled one.

There will never be another right of US entry of any kind for the exiled one.

13 - Declarations To Be Considered For Both Countries

1. The Nationality of the Exiled One.
   - US – Revocation of Citizenship
   - The Accepting nation – Declaration of Citizenship

2. Declaration of Citizenship Surrender.
   - US – Declaration of Revocation
   - The Accepting nation – Declaration of US Revocation

3. Clearance by all agencies.
   - US - Clearance of All Government Obligations
   - The Accepting nation – Specification of Acceptance Terms

4. Final Documentation and Details Needed.
   - US - Termination Effective Date and Time
   - The Accepting nation – Declaration of Citizenship

14 - Thank You

For
Considering
These
Ideas

And
I
Look
Forward
To
Reading
Your
Sharing

15 - Can You Help Carry A Message

Be A Messenger of Better Options

Things You Can Do

1. Develop patience, understanding, and plant seeds to a crop of possibilities.

2. Study the laws and ask questions.

3. Google Prison Reform Topics on the internet and read up on all the efforts out there and support those that you agree with.

4. Help the legal representatives of the people to understand what works and what does not.

5. Be respectful of the efforts of others.

6. Read about the struggles of the Correctional Authorities and advise options that you can see but they cannot.

7. Help the families of those who are incarcerated.

8. Look out for and support the children of those who are in prison.

16 - Can You Help Community Service

Be A Community Service Angel
Things You Can Share To Improve Quality of Life

1. Teach Parents to not buy Toy Guns that can get their child killed by mistake. Toy Guns Are Obsolete.

2. Help Addicts have a Prayer and a chance at http://AngelRaphaelSpeaks.com/Addicts-Prayer/

3. Help Alcoholics have a Prayer and a chance at http://AngelRaphaelSpeaks.com/Alcoholics-Prayer/

4. Help People Prepare for Health Care Emergencies http://angelraphaelspeaks.com/441-2/

5. Help Communicate & Save Lives with http://AngelRaphaelSpeaks.com/English-Language-Helper-Template-for-Non-English-Speakers/

6. Help Bring Peace to Troubled people by sending them to http://Create-A-Prayer.com

7. Help Reduce Stress at http://StressReleaseCoach.com

8. Help prisoners and their families find some peace at http://AngelRaphaelSpeaks.com/Prisons/

17 - Can You Help Communication Read and Advise Skills Needed

Things You Can Do Pro Bono

- If you read any of my messages and you have an opinion, I would love to hear it.

- If you read any of my messages and you have a clarification, I would love to hear it.

- If you read any of my messages and you have an idea, I would love to hear it.

- If you read any of my messages and you have an objection, I would love to hear it.

- If you read any of my messages and you have a comment, I would love to hear it.

- If you read any of my messages and you have a variation, I would love to hear it.

- If you read any of my messages and you have any of the above, I would love for you to write about it elsewhere also.

Volunteer Editors Welcome

Volunteer Beta Readers Welcome

18 - Don't Worry Ever

It Does Not Help Prayer Still Does!

Prayer Resource http://www.Create-A-Prayer.com

19 - Resource List

Distant Healing Sessions (or Join Mail List) – Write To mikewann@voicenet.com

Books by Rev. Mike at www.Amazon.com

Veterans Healing Six Pack
   Trauma Healing Options for VA Hospitals: Help for Veterans to Own Their Healing and their future.
   Trauma Healing Action Steps for Veterans: Help to Start Healing
   Trauma Healing Action Steps for Veterans: Empowerment
   Trauma Healing Action Steps for Veterans: Forgiveness
   Trauma Healing Action Steps for Veterans: Thought Freedom
   Tea For Veterans: Welcome One Home

PTSD Power Pack:
   The PTSD Project: Turn Pain To Power
   PTSD & Soul Retrieval: Putting One Back Together
   PTSD & The Purple PAD: Calling all Scientists and PTSD Patients

Angel Raphael Speaks Volume 1: Take Courage! God Has Healing in Store for You!
Angel Raphael Speaks Volume 2: Take Courage! God Has Healing in Store for You!
Angel Raphael Speaks Volume 3: Take Courage! God Has Healing in Store for You!
Angel Raphael Speaks Volume 4: Angels, Addicts, Alcoholics & Prisoners Oh Yeah!
Angel Raphael Speaks Volume 5: Prisoners Caring for Alcoholics - Australia In Miniature Projects Intro
Angel Raphael Speaks Volume 6: Prisoners Caring for Addicts - Australia In Miniature For Addicts
Reiki Journaling from Japan
Reiki Is Alive: God's Great Gift
Four Parts to Healing
Distant Healing: We Are All Connected

Stress Release Energy Work: How To Cope
Does Reiki Love Heal Cancer?
Group Consciousness
Salute To Philadelphia VA Medical Center: Thank You
Reiki Transcript for Reiki 2 & 3 Channels: Dr. Usui Is That You?
God Bless Kindle & Amazon
Puppies Are Different From People
If Your Dog Dies
Toy Guns Are Obsolete
Great Spirit Made Children With Red Skin: AND
The Cage of Fear: Is Not Locked
God Made Children Red, Yellow, Brown, Black & White: Greet Each Child With Kindness
Emergency Medical Kindness In The Cradle Of Liberty: Big City – Cracked Bell
Angels Are Always Around Addicts and Addicts: Help Is Near Now! Invit It In!
Angels Are Always Around Addicts and Alcoholics: Volume 2 - Tools To Help Re-Light Your Life
Prison Jobs Now: Providing Care For Addicts And Addicts
Controlled Care Communities Concept
Prison Possibilities Dialogue Series -Concept and Volumes 2, 3, 4, 5

Little Books at Kindle.com by Rev. Mike:
English Medical History Questionnaire For Non-English Speakers
English Language Helper For Non-English Speakers
Wise Wonderful Women Are The Well Of The Family
Answers for Test & Research: Dowsing Power
Crisis? Reiki! Baby? Reiki!
Bible References For Healing
Angel Raphael Speaks – Prisons
Angel Raphael Speaks – Veterans
The Saint Off Interstate 95

Angel Raphael Speaks through Rev. Mike Wanner. Please visit http://www.AngelRaphaelSpeaks.com or Facebook.com and Search for Angel Raphael Speaks

20 - Angels Please Prayers

Addict's
Angels of Healing Selected
Help Me to Stay Directed
Come To Me From The Sky
I Am Ready to Succeed Not Try
If I Don't Invite You In
I Might Not Win
I Have Been Lost For Too Long
Help Me To Stay Strong

Alcoholic's
Angels of Healing On High
Help Me to Stay Dry
Come To Me From The Sky
I Am Ready to Succeed Not Try
If I Don't Invite You In
I Might Not Win
I Have Been Lost For Too Long
Help Me To Stay Strong

From

http://AngelRaphaelSpeaks.com/AAAAAAA/

21 - Private Channeling

Angel Raphael Speaks is a series of free messages that are channeled through Reverend Mike Wanner for the Highest good and Highest Healing of all concerned.

Many questions arise about Reverend Mike doing private channeling and he does help with that so e-mail him.

Reverend Mike is available world-wide as a psychic channel, emotional release facilitator, spiritual energy practitioner & teacher, and public speaker. He looks forward to meeting you soon!

Email - mikewann@voicenet.com   215-342-1270

PRIVATE SPIRITUAL READINGS/channelings or Spiritual Healing Sessions: Telephone or in person. Rev. Mike is available for private, one-on-one intuitive sessions with you, his Guide Family, and your Guides. He helps by offering clarity on emotional situations about your life, your purpose, your spirituality, and the release of stuffed emotions and cellular memory.

Connect to the love of your Guides today!
Contact Rev. Mike for an appointment.

Sessions available:

Spiritual Readings
Angel Channeling
Distant Reiki Healing
Distant Clearing of Stuffed Emotions
Distant Clearing Cellular Memory
Distant Clearing Energy Blockages
Distant Clearing of the Chakras
Customized needs
Mastermind dowsing responses to yes/no direction finding questions.

Rev. Mike is a facilitator of healing. He brings you and the Divine together so that you can align with the Divine and have a great time and a great life. All healing is between you and God, as it should be. Go ahead and start without Rev. Mike. Visit his prayer site http://www.Create-A-Prayer.com. Take the first step NOW.

22 - Reverend Mike Wanner

Rev. Mike Wanner started his metaphysical and ministerial studies with Reiki in 1993 and has studied seven styles of Reiki in the U.S., Japan, Canada, Denmark and Australia. He is certified to teach. He became certified to teach Integrated Energy Therapy in 1999 and co-taught the first IET class of the new Millennium. Mike began dowsing in 2001.

Ordained as a Metaphysical Minister of the International Metaphysical Ministry and an Interfaith Minister of the Circle of Miracles Ministry, Rev. Mike practices and teaches spiritual energy therapies in the Philadelphia Area.

Rev. Mike holds ministerial degrees from the University of Metaphysics and the University of Sedona. He is a Pastoral Care Associate of Aria - Frankford Hospital. He taught at the National Academy of Massage Therapy and Health Sciences.

Rev. Mike was a faculty member of the Medical Mission Sister's Center for Human Integration's School of Integrated Body/Mind Therapies in Fox Chase, Philadelphia, PA for twelve years.

Rev. Mike is licensed by the teaching of Intuitional Metaphysics to practice Spiritual Healing and Scientific Prayer. Mike is also a Prayer therapist.

Rev. Mike was elected in 2007 to the status of "Fellow of the American Institute of Stress."

In 2008, Rev. Mike became a practitioner of Coincidental Recognition as he incorporated the CoRe system in to his spiritual healing practice.

In 2009, Rev. Mike trademarked a new healing process called Quantum Quatro! Subtle Energy System Support®.
In 2011, Rev. Mike joined the outreach program known as the Health Advantage Group.

In 2012, Rev. Mike became a Certified Professional Coach by The Master Coaching Academy and Joined The Personal Empowerment Group.

Prior to his metaphysical, ministerial and coaching studies, Rev Mike worked for Sears Roebuck and Co. while in High School and after graduation until he joined the U. S. Air Force in 1965 He returned to Sears from Vietnam in 1969 and stayed until 1978. His final Sears assignment was as an efficiency expert in Methods - Operational Research and Development.

He volunteered with Burholme Emergency Medical Services from 1969 and is still a Life Member and Board of Directors Member. He started a private ambulance company in 1975 and worked professionally in the field until 2001 when he devoted his full attention to real estate investing, healing, coaching and writing.

www.ReverendMikeWanner.com

www.ingramcontent.com/pod-product-compliance
Lightning Source LLC
Chambersburg PA
CBHW061238180526
45170CB00003B/1355